MW01133270

POPULAR PET CARE

Cats

Ann Larkin Hansen
ABDO & Daughters

Pets are more than just toys or playthings. They are part of our families. It is important to love and care for them. Popular Pet Care will help you understand your pet and know of its unique needs. Remember that your pet will depend on you to be responsible in caring for it.

Dr. David C. Hallstrom—Veterinarian

Published by Abdo & Daughters, 4940 Viking Drive, Suite 622, Edina, Minnesota 55435.

Cover Photo credits: Vik Orenstein
Interior Photo credits: Vik Orenstein, Peter Arnold, Inc., Wildwood Studio, Super Stock, Connie Bickman
Illustrations and Icons by: C. Spencer Morris

Edited by Julie Berg
Contributing editor Dr. David C. Hallstrom—Veterinarian

Special Thanks to our Popular Pet Care kids:
Peter Dumdei, Gracie Hansen, Brandon Isakson, Laura Jones, Annie O'Leary, Peter Rengstorf, Morgan Roberts, and Tyler Wagner.

Library of Congress Cataloging-in-Publication Data

Hansen, Ann Larkin.
      Cats / Ann Larkin Hansen.
      p.   cm. -- (Popular pet care)
      Includes index.
      Summary: Suggests what to consider in choosing a cat for a pet: then offers advice on how to understand, train, feed, and generally care for this amazing creature.
      ISBN 1-56239-780-X
      1. Cats--Juvenile literature. [1. Cats. 2. Pets.] I. Title. II. Series: Hansen, Ann Larkin. Popular pet care.
      SF445.7.H365   1997
      636.8--dc21   96-52999
                                                             CIP
                                                             AC

Contents

Why Have A Cat?

What could be more cozy on a cold night than a warm cat purring in your lap? Watching a **kitten** attack a paper bag will make anyone laugh. Having a cat in the house just makes it a friendlier place.

Cats are quiet. They don't take up much space, so they are great pets for people in apartments and small houses. And they don't need to be walked like a dog. Cats enjoy indoor living.

Kittens are cute and funny, but need more care. A grown cat is a better choice if you don't have much time for training and extra attention.

Opposite page: A cat and its owner.

Choosing A Cat

Cats come in all colors, shapes, and sizes. There are more than forty **breeds**, but most cats are just plain cats. A short-haired type is the easiest to care for. You can find a cat or **kitten** through ads in the paper, at a pet store, at an **animal shelter**, or when a neighbor's cat has kittens.

A cat or kitten should have clear eyes, clean pink ears, and a nose that isn't running. It should be friendly and playful. Take your time, and choose carefully! You may be living together for 12 or 15 years.

Opposite page:
New baby kittens can
put a smile on your face.

Before You Bring Your Cat Home

Are you ready for a new cat or **kitten**? Before you bring your cat home you must make a few preparations. Buy a **litterbox**, and fill it about two inches deep with **kitty litter**. This is the cat's bathroom. Put it somewhere handy, but private. Don't put it near feeding dishes.

Get two dishes that won't tip over, one for food and one for water. Have a basket or box with a soft towel for the cat's bed. Don't move the dishes or bed around. Cats like things to stay in the same place.

Put away knives, needles, medicines, and any other small things that could choke or poison a curious cat. Hide electric cords or tape them to the floor. Put plants out of the cat's reach—they could be poisoned if they eat them. Get a comb or brush to groom your cat, if it has long hair.

Brushing your cat is an important job.

The First Days
At Home

Cats don't like to be rushed. Give your new pet plenty of time to get used to its new home. Show it where the **litterbox** and food dishes are. If it will wear a **collar**, make sure it is partly made of elastic. Then if the collar gets caught on something, the cat can escape without strangling. **Kitten** collars must be changed every month or so as the kitten grows.

Never grab a cat by its leg or tail. Slide your hand under its ribs to lift it up. Make a cradle of your arms for the cat to rest in. When the cat wants to get down, always let go.

Opposite page: A girl cradling her kitten.

Understanding Your Cat

Cats are born to hunt. Like all good hunters, they are silent and quick. They are patient and very curious. They will explore every hole and corner in your house. Make sure you keep cupboards, dryers and garbage cans closed.

Cats like toys that they can pretend to hunt. Pull a thick piece of string or yarn past your cat and watch it attack! But don't let kitty attack your hands or ankles. The cat must learn it is not okay to bite people.

Most of a cat's time is spent sleeping or washing itself. Leave the cat alone if it does not want to play.

Cats are curious and like to play with things.

Training Your Cat

Cats don't like to take orders. They come and go as they please, and humans will never be able to change that. But there are some rules cats need to learn.

Cats should stay off counters and curtains. They should not steal human food. And they must not scratch the furniture. But hitting or yelling will not stop most cats. They will just wait until you're not around. Instead, squirt them with a squirt gun while they are doing something bad. Make sure they don't know where the water is coming from. Or you could put crinkled tinfoil on the counter, or something else your cat doesn't like. Then the cat won't want to be there.

Cats need to scratch to keep their claws healthy. Give your cat a **scratching post** that is as tall as it can reach. Cover it with carpet or burlap.

Cats need a scratching post to keep their claws healthy.

Feeding Your Cat

Dry cat food is usually best for your cat. **Kittens** need special **kitten chow**. Canned and semi-moist foods are good treats, but bad for cat teeth if they eat them all the time. Buy a good brand of food. Leave some out at all times, unless your cat is getting too fat. But do not let moist foods sit out for more than a half hour.

Cats love snacks and treats. A little warm milk is nice, but it gives some cats diarrhea. Cooked meats, cooked fish with no bones, cheese, and yogurt are all good for your cat. Don't give your cat chocolate, raw potatoes, dog food, or chicken bones.

Feeding your cat the right food is important.

Cat Housekeeping

The cat's **litterbox** must be cleaned every day. Scoop out the dirty litter and put it in the garbage. Add fresh litter. Once a week, take out all the old litter. If you don't keep the box clean, your cat probably won't use it.

Change the cat's water every day. Don't use soap on the dishes or litterbox, just wipe them out. Cats don't like strong soap smells and perfumes.

Take time every day to pet your cat and check for problems. If the cat goes outside, check it for **ticks**, **fleas**, dirty ears, and cuts.

It's important to change your cat's litterbox.

Spaying Or Neutering Your Cat

Spaying a female cat or **neutering** a male cat is an operation to keep them from having babies. Cats that are not spayed or neutered are a real headache for their owners. The males spray **urine** all over the house. They wander long distances, and get in loud fights. The females howl and yowl for up to three weeks at a time.

Many millions have to be put to death each year because there is no home for them. Don't add to the problem with more **kittens**. Have your **veterinarian** operate on your cat before it is six months old.

Opposite page: A veterinarian checking a cat for health problems.

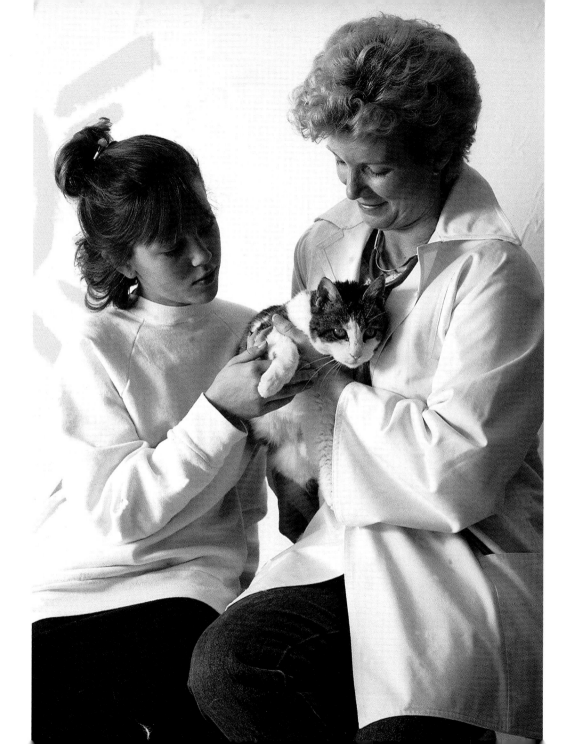

Living And Learning With Your Cat

Cats are easy pets. Changing food, water, and litter takes just a few minutes each day. Cats love to be petted, but they don't need lots of special attention. But one cat can get lonely if the family is gone all day. Maybe two cats is the answer!

Cats are amazing creatures. They smell, see, and hear much better than humans. They can jump and twist like no other animal. They have brains and personalities. You will learn a lot of things from your cat. But there is one question no one has ever been able to answer: do you own the cat, or does the cat own you?

Cats like to be petted and played with.

Keeping Your Cat Healthy

All **kittens** should be **vaccinated** before they are 12 weeks old. They need two shots, three or four weeks apart. This protects them against cat flu, distemper, and several other diseases. A **rabies** shot is given after three months of age, and is required by law. Older cats should have booster shots once a year.

Cats don't get sick much. But they do get **worms**, ear **mites**, eye infections, and all sorts of odd bumps and scrapes. Your **veterinarian** will show you what to look for. The vet will also show you how to trim the cat's claws.

When Your Cat Gets Old

By the time your cat is 10 or 12 years old, it will start to slow down. Your friend may be a little stiff, sleep more, and not be able to jump as high. Old cats may become blind, deaf, or have other problems. But with help from your **veterinarian**, you should be able to keep your cat comfortable and happy for quite a while.

But one day your cat won't be able to go on. You may find that it has quit eating, or can't get up any more. It may die quietly in its sleep. But if it doesn't, and it is suffering, you owe your old friend one last favor. Take it to the veterinarian and have the cat put "to sleep." This is a shot that will let your cat die painlessly.

You can have your cat buried in a pet cemetery, but this is very expensive. Most owners have their pets cremated, or have the **veterinarian** take care of the body.

You can be proud of yourself if your pet had a good life and gentle handling. Maybe soon you may be ready for another pet.

Your cat will always be a good friend.

Glossary

Animal Shelter: A place that cares for lost and unwanted pets. Because there are so many unwanted cats and dogs, homes can not be found for most of the animals at shelters.

Breed: Different kinds of an animal. Some popular cat breeds are Persian and Siamese.

Collar: A band worn around the neck. Often bells or tags are hooked on the collar.

Flea: A tiny biting insect that lives on the cat and makes the cat itchy.

Kitten: A cat under one year old.

Kitten Chow: Food especially for kittens. Kittens need more nutrients in their diet than full-grown cats.

Kitty Litter: Small sandy or papery pellets sold in bags. Put in litterbox to soak up the cat's messes.

Litterbox: A plastic basin, like a dishpan, that the cat uses as a bathroom. Most cats know how to use a litterbox and do not have to be trained.

Mites: Tiny insects that live on the cat, usually in the ears. The ears will look dirty and greasy inside when the cat has mites.

Neuter: An operation done on a male cat to keep it from fathering kittens.

Rabies: An incurable disease of mammals, including cats and humans. Rabies is extremely dangerous.

Scratching Post: A post or piece of log mounted on a base to keep it standing upright. The post is covered with carpet or burlap bags for the cat to sink its claws into.

Spay: An operation done on a female cat to keep it from having kittens.

Tick: Insects that bite and hang on for several days while they suck an animal's blood. Ticks carry many diseases, and can create sore spots.

Urine: Liquid waste.

Vaccinate: To give a shot that will prevent certain diseases.

Veterinarian: An animal doctor.

Worms: Tiny worms that live inside an animal and can make it sick. There are many different kinds.

Index